22 Messages from the Archangels

Deborah Lloyd

Illustrations © 2017 by Cristina Găvănescu

Copyright

© 2017, Acorn Gecko SRL

ALL RIGHTS RESERVED. This book contains material protected under International and Federal Copyright Laws and Treaties. Any unauthorized reprint or use of this material is prohibited. No part of this book may be reproduced or transmitted in any form or by any means, electronic or mechanical, including photocopying, recording, or by any information storage and retrieval system without express written permission from the publisher.

Table of Contents

The Story of This Book 5
An Introduction to the Archangels 9
Messages from Metatron *13*
   Message #1 from Metatron 15
   Message #2 from Metatron 22
   Message #3 from Metatron 28
Messages from Raphael *35*
   Message #1 from Raphael 37
   Message #2 from Raphael 43
   Message #3 from Raphael 50
Messages from Zadkiel *55*
   Message #1 from Zadkiel 57
   Message #2 from Zadkiel 62
   Message #3 from Zadkiel 67
Messages from Ariel *73*
   Message #1 from Ariel 75
   Message #2 from Ariel 80
   Message #3 from Ariel 86
Messages from Uriel *91*
   Message #1 from Uriel 93
   Message #2 from Uriel 99
   Message #3 from Uriel 104
Messages from Gabriel and Michael *111*
   Message #1 from Gabriel 113
   Message #1 from Michael 119
   Message #2 from Gabriel 123
   Message #2 from Michael 128
   Message #3 from Gabriel 134
   Message #3 from Michael 140

Final Message - One Voice *147*
   One Voice *149*
About Deborah Lloyd... *153*

The Story of This Book

The angels have always been a part of my life. As a little girl raised in a Catholic family, we learned about the angels and said a daily prayer to our guardian angels. I talked to my guardian angel frequently; she was like a best friend. Angels have always been real for me, and I believe angels have always protected me. Sometimes, this was as concrete as not stepping off a curb into the path of an oncoming car; or, helping me to find the right words in a difficult situation. I love reading books composed of angel stories – those books where people share their own stories of an encounter with an angel.

My connection to angels grew even stronger when I learned Reiki, over fifteen years ago. The energy healing modality of Reiki is a method of bringing Universal Life Force Energy into a person's being, promoting relaxation and healing. Simply put, Reiki changed my life! Not only did I experience physical improvements in symptoms resulting from post-polio syndrome, but I also expanded my knowledge and understanding of the true interconnectedness between physical, emotional/mental and spiritual aspects of myself. I explored other ways of understanding the Divine Spirit, including shamanic journeying, yoga, mediumship, and others. I grew in my own intuitive abilities. During Reiki sessions with clients, I received messages – from deceased relatives, Spirit Guides, Ascended Masters, the Wise Council, and yes – the angels. I never know who will show up – but it is always the right Spirit Being, with the right message – for the client.

My connection to the angels has grown stronger over time. Then, I was instructed to write these messages from the Archangels, one at a time. With their guidance, I started each session with a little ritual of spending meditative time with a few angelic items I own. I felt the connectedness with the angels.

Then, I sat down in front of my laptop, closed my eyes and let the words flow. That is right – I was guided to keep my eyes closed (thank goodness, I am a fast typist!).

For me, it is necessary to close my eyes during meditation, Reiki sessions, and times when I want to get connected, and stay connected, to Spirit Beings. I am easily distracted by seeing things in whatever setting I am in, and my mind can easily veer off the meditative state. So, the Archangels told me to close my eyes and simply type what they say. It was that simple.

This is a channeled book – in other words, the messages are not written by me. The Archangels said these words, in my mind, and I typed away. I remained conscious during these times. Amazingly (or not), I was never interrupted with phone calls or other intrusions.

At times, I felt surprised by their words – and by the alternating messages of Gabriel and Michael - but immediately set aside my thoughts. I did not want to interrupt the flow of words or insert any of my thoughts. Also, I did not reread any of the messages until all were completed. I did not change the messages, in any way. You will read what I received.

To say I feel humbled by this experience is an understatement. I have learned much from other channeled books, and presentations by people who channel spirits – I never dreamed I would do the same one day. My heart is full of gratitude for living this experience of being a vessel for channeling. Likewise, the Archangels are pleased that you have found this book and will spend time reading it and meditating on the messages. This book is written for your spiritual growth.

An Introduction to the Archangels

(This introduction is channeled.)

We, the Archangels, greet you and give you honor for choosing to read our messages. We ask you to work with us as you are willing and able. We ask you to set aside any earthly concerns for short periods of time, to sit with this book and more importantly, to sit with the messages as these were dictated to this author. We ask that you meditate, or journal, as you see fit. This will help you on your spiritual path. This will aid in changing the energies on the earth, as this is so needed at this point in earthly time. Also, many changes are occurring on earth, and it is the work of all people to participate in making this a positive change. This will affect all peoples and all living creatures on earth. It will also affect Mother Earth herself.

We will speak to you individually for most of the messages, but we will blend as one for the last message. We ask you to listen to our individual voices. We each have a strong energy, with varying emphases. Yet, we are One. This is the same as your energies. All people have individual characteristics, with certain strengths and energies. Yet, you are One People. We have the same make-up in that regard.

You will hear the differences in our voices, and in our tones, and even the words we use. This too is like all people. No two people are alike in every aspect. The angels are the same.

The Archangels have chosen this time to be especially strong and vocal in our communications with people on the earth plane. This is due to the fact that there are cosmic changes happening right now. The energetic vibrations of people will help to determine the final outcomes.

We do not say these words to make you fearful. No, we say these words to help you manifest a greater good, a better outcome. Please know the Mother Earth will not be destroyed, but she may still have more harm done to her, if things do not change quickly.

Let us use one example. Most of you do believe in global climate change. It is real. There are still some non-believers, however. If the believers use their voices and their power, climates can be reversed, to the good. It will be your choice in how involved, or non-involved, you become. Free will is still a gift from God to all of you, and to us also. There is still time to make the right choices, but you do have to act quickly. There is only the present moment, and you can use your free will to act accordingly.

One of the main points of this book is to remind you of our continual assistance, and our love. We will always support you. All you have to do is ask. We will be reminding you of this over and over again.

When you read this book, please ask for our assistance during your reading time and your meditation time. If there is something you do not understand, please ask. If there is something that troubles you, please ask us for further clarification. Communicating to you in spoken language has its limitations. Our wisdom, and your wisdom, do not have these limitations. Sometimes, it is difficult to express our messages in words. You know how difficult this can be at times. It is difficult to express exactly what you mean, the meaning goes beyond words. We will do our best to convey the essence of each message.

We ask that you approach this book with patience and with openness. We ask you to revisit this book over and over again. We assure you, you will find new meanings and deeper understanding every time you read a message over. This is not meant to be read one time only. This is meant to be re-read, so that you can grasp full, and new, meanings. It is not unlike other religious works that you may know. Every read will bring new understandings.

May we remind you, we will be with you every time you read a message from this book. We will be with you every time you strive to bring healing energies onto the Earth. We are always with you.

We love and honor you.

Messages from Metatron

Message #1 from Metatron

I AM Archangel Metatron. I am here to assist you and your readers on how to become closer to God. I am a teacher and I will guide you all the way. I come to earth now because I am needed by you. You must expand. You must learn more. I am here to teach you All That Is.

I once lived among you on earth. So, I understand what it is like to be on earth. But you can also understand what it is like here in the heavenly realms. It is the same and it is different.

I am Light and you are light. All beings are made of light. Your light can shine on earth but you do not believe that is so. It is so. All of you are being called to shine your light now. Your earth is full of darkness and your light is needed more than ever. You must shine your light in order to save the world.

There is a darkness that has been allowed to spread over all your lands. This darkness though can be changed to light and to glory. You are not defeated yet, but you could be defeated if you allow yourselves to be defeated. It is that simple.

Please have faith. Faith is very important in today's world. People are forgetting there is a Divine Being who always is with them and is always protecting them. But, they continue to work against the Divine, rather than working in accordance with Him.

I am Metatron. I am here to help you today and every day you live on earth. Please do not forget this. It is very important. You must stay connected to the Spirit realms. You cannot live in harmony with your earth if you have separated from us. You must stay connected and do not forget about us. We are here to help.

Why I am coming to you through this book is to give you messages. This writer has said yes to me. I want all of you to say yes to your part in saving the earth - in healing yourselves, healing each other and healing for the earth. Each of you has a specific role in doing this. But, you are marching around like little lost soldiers with no roles and no goals. You have bought into the modern world's way of thinking. It is time to leave that behind you. Changes must be made. Priorities must change. You can do this; you have to do this.

This is a plea. This is a plea for you to make changes before it is too late. Your earth is beautiful, but you do not take the time to see the beauty. You are always in a rush, always in a hurry. Slow down and take the time to live according to your soul's desire. Take the time to read my words and to let them sink into your soul. Take the time to reorder your life and get your priorities right. It is important that you do so. As you grow in this journey, it will become easier and easier. I know that you need to eat and you need to pay bills. But it can be much simpler. You are making your lives so hard because you have it backwards.

People think I am a very serious angel, but I also have a sense of humor. I can laugh along with you. We will be learning some hard things and some fun things. We angels like to have fun, you know. We can laugh together as we learn how upside down all of us have had things for many ages.

I am also the archangel for wisdom and for reaching you on earth. We like to have synchronicities, those things that seem like coincidences but they are not. We like to startle you from time to time. This is to help you wake up and see there is more to life than your jobs. Jobs are necessary sometimes, but you are too wrapped up in them. So, we make a funny thing happen. You are amazed. It is a sign that there is another whole life out there that you so often ignore. It is important for you to stop and connect with Spirit.

You must remember that you are from these realms too. You have these realms within you right now, but you are too busy to see it. You go about your daily business and do not remember to connect. We will spend time together being connected to each other. We will learn many important things together. You will grow in your beliefs. You will grow in grace.

Deborah will be taking down these messages, one at a time. I ask you to read them, one at a time. Do not rush through this book. Rather, I want you to read one and meditate on it for a day or two. Please find the messages for you within the message. Different people will see different things, because that is what is needed in their life right now.

This is the first of many messages, but within each message there are many messages. Whenever you read a new message, sit silently in your room, while you read it and for some time after you finish reading. Some of you will want to reread the message, and that will be good for you. You will find new messages for you each time you read it, whether it is the same day, or another day in the future.

I will be working with each of you individually and with you collectively. There is great energy in group work. That is why church communities can be good. The group prayer is very dynamic and powerful. When you read, and reflect on the messages, your energy is joining forces with the energies of other people.

Please know this book is not the only way for me, or the other angels, to work with you. But, it is a book that is in your hands right now, so you have chosen this way to work with me, right now. That is good. I ask that you finish this program. You will be lead to other programs, other ways, of receiving messages. For some, this book will be one of the first ways they have of connecting with me and the other angels. For others, it will be preceded by other methods. What is important is that you follow your path. Everyone is on different paths.

We show people paths, but it is always your choice to say yes or no. We like to invite people, through thought and signs and other ways, to try something that will be helpful to them to grow spiritually. Because of free will, a special gift from God to people on earth, you always have the choice to say yes or no to us and to all spirits.

As time goes on, I will be showing myself to people all over the world. Some archangels have been in touch with humanity for many centuries. I have been less involved as people were not ready for my knowledge. They would not understand my messages. I work in higher realms of understanding. People on earth call this esoteric wisdom, but actually it is just a higher plane of understanding. There are many levels and human beings are learning more of them.

Souls have evolved over time, and more evolved souls are on earth right now. You made the choice to return to earth now because of the major work that needs to be done. There are many healers and enlightened people on earth presently, because this difficult work needs to be done, in order to save Mother Earth.

Living in both spirit world and in the earth world is something all of you are called to do. It is possible to live in this duality, but actually it is nonduality. The two worlds exist simultaneously, and they are not separate, they are connected. They exist in the same space and in the same time. There is no division between space and time, although it is difficult to see when you only know the earth aspects of this. More and more of you are learning this is the case.

When you read my words, you will need to do things to stay grounded. It is best to ground yourself by firmly planting your feet on the ground, sitting up straight and staying consciously aware. You may need to eat something after you read a message. That is fine. Your physical body energy is heavy and these messages have an etheric quality to them. We do not want you to float away - that is humor.

I love each and every person on earth. There are many lost souls on earth, and we want you to help us to bring them back into the fold. It is like the story of the Master Jesus being the shepherd bringing the sheep back into the fold. All people will have the opportunity to come back to knowledge and wisdom. They will have a choice though. All you can do is ask for them to join us. It will be their decision.

I will leave you now.

Many blessings to you as you approach this work.

Message #2 from Metatron

I am your friend. I am here to help you and support you in all your work and during all your days. I am not a stranger. Rather, I am someone who knows you very well. I know your thoughts and I know your intentions. I know what you are doing at all times. But do not worry. I do not judge you. You judge yourselves. You know when you are living in the Light and when you are not. I do not need to tell you that information.

I am here to help you live your life purpose. Your soul came into the earth plane this time for a very specific reason. You have life goals and it matches what your soul needs during this lifetime. It is easy to discern this goal as we are helping you to discover it. It would be easier if we just told you in a telegram or a letter. But your discovering your life goal is an important part of your growth.

You have to learn to listen to your soul messages. You need to connect with us and with other spirits to figure it out. If we simply told you, you would not have this opportunity to learn it for yourselves. It is like not giving a child an answer to a mathematics question. The child needs to figure it out, so they learn how to figure out future mathematic problems. In the same way, you need to learn how to access all the mysteries your soul contains.

Your soul has all the memories and life experiences that you have already lived. Some people call this the akashic records, but you do not have to learn akashic record-reading. You need to spend quiet time to learn how to talk with your soul. That is all you have to do. If you are having a hard time with this, please ask for my help. I can nudge you in the right direction.

You have to learn to trust the thoughts in your mind, when they are given to you by the angels and other spirits. You think it is your imagination. It is and it is not. You see imagination as a whimsical thing, something that is not true. Instead, we use your imagination to communicate with you.

We work with creative people in using their imagination. We have shown ourselves to artists in their minds and they draw us the way we showed ourselves to them. We work with

writers and ask them to use their gift of imagination to communicate with you. Sometimes, we channel ourselves directly, like we are doing here.

So, the imagination is one tool we use to talk with you. You only limit yourselves if you believe there is only one way to communicate with us. We use many ways, and we are a large group of many spirits. Some people on earth connect more with angels, some with animal spirits and some with deceased relatives. The list goes on. No one way is better than any other way. You relate to the spirits that are most comfortable and familiar to you. This goes back many lifetimes. Sometimes, you start to relate to an unfamiliar spirit because you realize that spirit may have new messages for you, or a new way of seeing things. Thank you for being open and trusting. It is not easy to connect with a spirit that is unknown to you. It can be very beneficial though.

All of you have important lessons to learn. That is why you chose such a difficult time to come to earth. These are the most challenging of times. There is much greed and destructive ways of thinking right now. It is not easy to hear all these things happening all over the world.

At the same time, there are many good things happening due to the presence of many lightworkers. They continue to come in, in large numbers. Most babies have lived many lives, and they have chosen to come back to help move mankind to a place of loving peace.

We are your friends. We come to you in love and peace. We can assist you to find solutions to the world's problems. Ask what you can do. If each person did this, peace would manifest. Each person has a role. Do not think you are insignificant. Nothing is further from the truth. The truth is that each life makes a difference. In fact, every minute of your life, and every thought in your head, makes a difference.

Each thought creates an energy that is either full of love, or full of fear. Each thought creates a ripple effect. What is happening on earth right now is based in fear. When people become fearful, they can make bad decisions. And they may not love their neighbor.

You can create a Christ consciousness on earth. Christ consciousness is simply the love of the ascended Master Jesus. Jesus has the highest form of love and compassion. If each person tuned into his energy, there would only be peace and love and compassion on earth.

There would be no room for fear, hate and violence. It would disappear. That is your goal, to become an instrument of love, every day, all the time.

You can ask for help to become aware of your thoughts. If you start to have a fearful thought, we can help you to catch it and change it before it is formed. You can transmute all your thoughts and never have a negative energy thought again. How amazing that would be!

This is a hard task when there is so much negative energy swirling around you. But it is possible to transform your thoughts and this will make it easier for others to do the same. Can you imagine being totally surrounded by loving thoughts only? What a lovely world it would be. As some of you would call it, it would be "heaven on earth."

Heaven is not a place of golden streets and pearly gates. It is a place of total peace and love. You can establish it on earth, but you have a long way to go to reach it. It is possible.

The Christ did not have negative thoughts. He only had love in his heart for all people. He came to earth to show it is possible to live in this manner. It is also possible for you to live this way. You must believe this. It is attainable. There are some people on earth right now who live this way. You too can reach this goal, it is attainable.

We are your friends. A friend always goes out of the way to show their love and support. We will do everything we can, all you have to do is ask.

We embrace you every day of your lives. We hold you in our arms. Have you ever felt as if someone was around you and you looked, and no one was there? That was one of us. We do not jump out at you, we would scare you. But we do whisper in your ears, or make a humming sound. Sometimes, we appear as flashes of light when you close your eyes. Some people have the gift of seeing us. But, if everyone saw us, there would be no need for faith or trust. We remain unseen as this helps your growth the most.

Again, please listen to your inspirational thoughts. Do not dismiss them or think you made it up. You did not. We are near you at all times. We communicate with you often, but often you do not notice.

We love you. We are your friends.

Message #3 from Metatron

Today we will talk about miracles. There are miracles around you, all the time. Often, you do not see them or recognize them as miracles. Or, you think they only happen to other people. This is because you do not believe you are worthy of having a miracle. That is not true. All human beings are worthy of the unconditional love that is always there for them. All people are worthy to have miracles in their lives.

There are many wonderful miracle stories. Please learn about these and you will see miracles happen to people who may have thought they were not worthy either. God does not judge you as you judge yourselves. God loves all people and all people may receive a miracle.

Miracles are God's way of shifting energy in the world. Just when things may seem desperate or hopeless, He reminds you that nothing is hopeless. He can change anything for you. You do not have to ask for miracles. If it is meant to be, God will grant them to you.

You often think of miracles as a cure or something related to medicine. There are miracles of physical healing. But other kinds of miracles exist too.

There are miracles of awakening. A person can be going through life half asleep and one day something happens to awaken that person. Usually it is something quite unexpected. That too is a miracle. Perhaps, you have had a miracle in your own life, just like that. Thank God for your own personal miracles.

When you have your own miracle, it is good for you to share with other people. This can be an awakening for them. You can show them how to become aware of miracles in their own lives. People sharing their stories with others is an important way to learn the messages of God. He works through other people.

Have you ever thought perhaps I should share this experience with someone? Then, you become scared and fearful of what their reaction might be. So, you say nothing. That was a missed opportunity for you, and more importantly, for the person who did not get to hear your story. Have courage. Do not be afraid.

Fear is one reason why the earth is in the trouble it is in. The earth would be better if more people shared their experiences with others. Again, let me say, this is one important way to learn the Truth. Each of you has an obligation to share your stories with other people. You will discover how any others have had similar experiences to yours, and that will help your faith and your beliefs too.

There is a reason why community is vitally important on earth. People were not made to live in isolation and in fear. People were made for their souls to learn important lessons and important truths. God has given you many ways to learn these truths, and miracles are one way. Miracles are a lovely expression of God's unconditional love.

Miracles can also come in the form of healing, on all levels of human existence. All people are wounded in some way, whether it is physical, emotional or feeling disconnected from the Source. A miracle can be the path to healing. There is not one form of healing, but rather many forms. People are drawn to one form or another. All healing paths are good.

Miracles also exist in what you would call the everyday things of life. Look outdoors. All the plants, trees, air, sun, animals, and everything is nature is a miracle. A tree starts from a little seed and years later, it can be tall, strong, and sturdy. The baby's life too is a miracle. Find the miracles in your everyday life.

Miracles are simply reminders of God's love for you. Sometimes, we are called for assistance in making these miracles occur. We might place an item on the chair for you to see, or have you turn the wrong way on a road to see a sign with a message on it for you, or something similar to this.

There are some things that we commonly drop for someone to see. The white feather, a penny - or we might send a butterfly to circle around your head. Again, small reminders of the eternal Source are being sent to you.

You may pray for a miracle, and your prayers are always answered in some way. Someone may not be cured from a terminal disease, though, because it is not part of their life purpose for the disease to disappear. But, they may find peace and happiness on the journey. Or, they may say something to a doctor or nurse that helps them to be different in their practice. Or, they may become an example of grace to family and friends, or to another patient.

The miracles we enjoy are the unexpected ones. These are real wake-up calls. The surprise element is part of the awakening process.

You will find that as your belief in miracles grows, you will experience more miracles in your life. Or, is it that you are now just seeing and recognizing them for what they are? This is a question for you to ponder.

Miracles are a way to stay connected to God and to all spirits. It is so easy to get entangled in your earthly life that you forget there are spiritual realms where you may connect. You can experience the beauties of the peace and harmony that exist in these realms, even when you are living in the dense earth energies.

Miracles are like a breath of fresh air, on a sultry, heavy day. The earth's energies can be heavy, and miracles can bring Light into these vibrations. Try to become less tangled up in your daily concerns, and open your minds to this other reality. It is there all the time, waiting for you to be with us.

We always welcome your company and your awareness of us. We also welcome your awareness and gratitude for all the gifts that are bestowed upon you. If you could see all of it, you would constantly be expressing gratitude and love.

We are always with you and we love you.

Messages from Raphael

Message #1 from Raphael

Blessings to you! I am Raphael, and I am here to teach you about unconditional love and healing. So many of you do not love yourselves, and that is changing everything around you. Please know that you are always, always loved, no matter what you do.

Many of you do not think you are worthy of this kind of love. This is not true. God made you and He has always loved you, from your first life until this lifetime. And, He will love you forever.

If you could learn to love yourselves in this way, you would never have any problems. You would accept whatever happened to you in peace, knowing that it was important for your soul's journey. Instead, you take it upon yourselves to see yourselves as less worthy. That is a fallacy.

Healing is simply self-acceptance. When you learn to accept yourself as a lovable, and loving, human being, everything shifts. Your energy changes, and you are on the path to healing.

Healing is always available to you. It is already inside you, but you do not see it. You do not even believe it is possible. All you have to do is become aware of it, recognize it. Once you do that, healing energies breaks through the self-constructed walls that you built around your heart and around your soul. There is no need for you to do that. God did not put up walls, you did.

My purpose and my mission is to bring healing into the world. It is done one person at a time, although I can be working with many people at one time. This is hard for you to understand as you only know how time exists on earth.

Our spiritual time does not exist, it is different. In the same way, we are able to be many places at one time.

I often join those people who bring healing to others. I have worked with Deborah many times, and I have shown myself to her. This is because she perceived a spirit was with her. Often, I work with people who do healing work, but many do not perceive my presence. I will continue to give them signs that I am at their side. Sometimes, I place my hands over their hands, intensifying their work. It hastens the healing. It makes it more powerful. Remember, two beings are always stronger than one.

I work with doctors and nurses and all those who provide care to the sick. Many of them do not perceive my presence as they are stuck in their scientific minds. Eventually, some awaken to the possibility there is a greater power working with them, as science only cannot explain the miracles they see. I, and other angels, work in all the hospitals and medical settings in the world. We go to car accidents and natural tragedies, helping the sick and injured. Some of us help those who die to move to the next plane. This is also healing, because sudden deaths can be disorienting, and the soul feels confused and lost. We take them to the Light.

We are greatly pleased when a person seeks healing, no matter the form. Some prefer the medical approach, some energy healing, others talk to a therapist, the list goes on. We are present in all these places. We may whisper in the professional's ear, or we may give them a thought to consider. We are very pleased when they take our advice because we understand a bigger perspective. This will help the patient to become better.

Please be warned: Healing does not mean we always cure. That cannot happen on earth. People become sick for many reasons, but one of the main reasons is that it is a way to leave the earth plane and transition to another plane. If there was no sickness, people would have to find other ways to leave the earth.

Also, sicknesses are used to teach the soul lessons. You chose to come to earth to live out difficult circumstances so your soul could learn lessons. Deborah works with people who are dying, and she can tell you many people learn the greatest life lessons as they prepare to die and leave the earth. This is not connected to religious practice necessarily. Many lessons are taught about the value of life on earth, loss, beliefs about eternity, and so many more. It would be good for people to learn these lessons throughout their lifetimes and not wait until the last days. It is much easier.

I, Raphael, love to work through people's hands. Hands connect you, one to another. We angels also can form hands, to touch you in more focused ways. When I form hands, to place over a person's healing hands, there is a strong connection and the healing energies intensify greatly. We are careful not to give too much energy, it can feel overwhelming to a human body. We are able to control the amounts, depending on the person and his energy field.

We have been involved with humankind over many, many centuries. There have been many inspired art works, prayers and writings about us. We are always present. The more you become aware of us, the more you will be able to feel our helping hands.

I often work with heart energies. The heart is very important to you in maintaining life on earth and in expressing all your emotions. Many people have heart problems, because they are either blocking or suppressing their emotions. Or, they find their emotions too difficult to deal with. This can lead to physical heart problems. It is all connected.

When I place my hands on your heart, please know I am only sending unconditional love. If you feel this love, everything else falls into place. Jesus also works with your heart energies. His Sacred Heart can send energy directly into your heart. He sends His love to you, always. He brings a strength and power unlike any other spiritual being. We honor Him all the time, as should you. He is the great Teacher and the great Lover. We honor Him.

If you feel lonely, call me to be with you. If you feel hurt or sad, call on me. If you feel abandoned or neglected, call on me. Remember, you are never alone. I and the other spirits are always there, ready to be called upon. We do not always wait for an invitation, but it is good for you to be aware of our presence and our abilities and gifts. We were formed to help you. That is our mission. Please call upon us.

I am leaving now. I am ready to be at your side, bringing love and healing into your life. It is always available.

Peace to you and your loved ones on earth.

Message #2 from Raphael

Let us explore the many reasons why you do not get the things you desire when you wish for them. One reason is Divine Timing. Everything in the Universe happens according to plan. Often, you are not cured from a disease because the timing is not right. This may be due to another person needing to learn a lesson, or the other person has not yet taken an action that would enable your disease to be cured. Sometimes, the timing is simply not right for you. You need to learn more lessons from the disease.

We do not judge you based on whether or not you are able to be freed from the effects of disease. Judgment does not exist with us. Only you can be the judge of your own thoughts and your actions. We are here to always love you and to guide you. You make your own decisions and you take your own actions. That is free will.

If you feel distressed by a disease or an injury, please try to change your thoughts. Try to accept this injury and then you will see the many gifts that are there for you. I know this is difficult when you may be in pain, or are experiencing other suffering. Remember there are gifts in everything you have. There are blessings in everything you experience, although it may seem negative at the time you are experiencing it.

One of the most important lessons for everyone on earth to learn is the value of each experience, each day of your life. When you go through life not being aware, it is a lost opportunity to grow in love. It is like walking through a large field of beautiful wildflowers. Some people do not notice the wildflowers. Rather, they tramp them down and do not see the beauty. Challenges in your lives are like the beautiful flowers. They seem annoying, or seem to be in your way to a happy life, but instead they are part of the plan to create a happy and beautiful life. You must see them in a new perspective.

Diseases and injuries are also opportunities to experience healing in a whole way. You may think of healing as a cure for disease, but healing is much broader than that. Healing is recognizing the healing energies that are already within you. God made you into a perfect human being, and that also includes your physical body. People tend to misuse and abuse their bodies. Many decisions made on earth have been harmful to the human body. If all nature was pure and whole, there would be no disease. But, many decisions of greed and selfish desires have affected the planet. People have to eat food that is full of harmful substances. Even the waters are not healthy for people. Yet, the human body needs these substances for nourishment. Do you understand how these decisions made over the centuries are affecting you now? We recognize there are now some efforts being made to clean up these substances. It is not too late, but the time is near. Take action now.

So, healing is already your birthright. Each person on earth has the right to be healthy and whole, in all aspects of their being. There does not need to be physical maladies, emotional or mental illnesses, or even spiritual distancing from God. All of these things are present on earth, only because people do have free will, and many bad decisions have been made. Each person has implanted in their souls the desire to be healthy and whole.

Look at the many ways people try to get healthy again. People exercise, try to get calm, and they try to connect to Spirit. This is good. Every time a person makes an effort to become whole again, it is a step in the right direction. It is reconnecting to something that is already in the soul. It is not a change really. Rather, it is a remembering of what the original plan for people is. There was no plan for all this suffering and illness and destruction. The body was made to be whole, just as the soul is always whole.

Afflictions of the soul are a distancing from the unconditional love of God. But, the soul does not suffer permanent damage. Rather, it moves away from God, but it remains whole. The soul never forgets its connection to God. The human mind, however, can override the soul's great desire to remain with God at all times. It is being neglected, but it is not being harmed. In Divine Time, the soul will be fully reconnected to God at some time.

You can make efforts now to help that reconnection. We give you many signs when you are on the right path. We can bring healing into your lives, to help you remember the pure bliss of feeling the reconnection to God. It is pure bliss. Once you experience it, you will not want to leave.

One tool we use is the near-death experience. When people transition from earthly life, they approach this pure bliss. Sometimes, people are sent back to earth as their life purpose was not yet achieved. Those people have been coming forward more and more to teach the lessons of that spiritual connection. That is the main purpose for their return. It is a tool for us to teach people about the next planes of existence.

Healing is already implanted in your soul and in your heart. We see many people making efforts to heal. Sometimes, they go from one healer to another. Let us repeat. No person on earth is truly a healer, but what they do is help a person to find their own healing. It can seem magical to the person who finds healing. But, the healing was there all along, they just did not see it. Their lack of awareness did not make it possible.

When a person believes healing is possible, a new level of possibilities is achieved. Sometimes, they can sit in quiet meditation, and their awareness will help the healing to occur. Sometimes, they need another person to work with. The healing facilitator, through kindness and love, and through certain actions, can bring a healing into existence. It is a creative process.

Again, let me remind you a person may not get exactly what they hope for. Their life plan may need to include a certain disease, for the remainder of their life on earth. There may be other plans for that person, and others in his circle, for the existence of the disease. The disease will disappear at some point, but it may be after the transition of this life to the next.

When a human body moves to the next plane, no diseases exist. It is true. Those who cannot walk will walk again. Those who do not remember anything will remember again. Those who do not have compassion will have to return to earth and try to learn compassion again. Their souls will not elevate to a higher plane until this most important lesson is learned. Many with physical afflictions will be able to move to higher planes as they have learned the lessons of the affliction. Frequently, those with afflictions are the most compassionate people on earth! It is true.

There are very few people on earth, right now, who are in a state of being fully healed and whole. There a few people, however. Some are working in their own circles, and some are quite well-known. Look around you and see the people who are almost fully healed; their numbers are much greater. They are influenced some by the heavy dense energies of earth and all the toxics on earth. These people are great teachers, as they strive to live a life of love, harmony and peace. Seek them out, as you will learn from them. Ask yourselves, when you are affected deeply by someone, the real reasons for this. Does this person emanate a strong energy of love and compassion? Do they live peace? Is this a person you should model your life after? If so, look for the lessons they are living. It will help you in your spiritual reconnection to the One.

Healing is simply knowing you are whole, in the eyes of God. I will work with you in finding healing in your life. That is my main purpose. I bring love and calmness and peace into your being. I place my hands upon you. I touch your heart. I love you with great compassion. I see how hard life on earth can be. There is a greater Energy, however. This Energy can replace all the hurts and challenges of your lives.

May it be so.

Message #3 from Raphael

You are powerful because you have the powerful and unconditional love of the One. This love already lives within you, and it is available so that you may show this kind of love in the world, towards other people and towards yourself. Many of you doubt that you are worthy of this love, but that is not true. All human beings have this unconditional love.

You are a child of God. Remember the love you felt as a newborn baby. It was purely unconditional. Anything you did, your parents still loved you. God's love is like that. There is nothing you can do that will take away this love. It is always there.

This love, when recognized and lived out, brings much power into the earth's sphere. It can permeate everything. If everyone lived with this knowledge, there would be no more hate and no more wars in the world. But, people do not think they are worthy of this love. So, they seek love and power in other ways. These ways do not produce the love they seek, it is an illusion. But, they continue to pursue it anyways.

All people have the need for this kind of love. Parents really try to give it to their children, and some do very well at showing this love. Other parents do not know how to love this way because they never received it from their parents. Nor, were they taught this kind of love is present in their loves through God. In fact, they may have been taught the opposite – that they were not good enough to be loved. This is a grave sin for parents if they did not teach their children they are always loved.

I see your reaction to the word "sin." I know that sin has been represented to you through many churches and religions. Sin is not living in the truth and love of God. People should not feel guilty about this. Anytime you do not live in the Truth of God, you could have done better. You always had the choice. What you need to do is recognize this sin, this omission, and then change it. You should not feel guilty. You should learn from it and resolve not to live in untruth again.

There is too much guilt in the world. Guilt does not need to exist, it is a negative energy. It does not help people. What helps people, when they have committed a wrong, is to acknowledge it and move forward in love and light. Sometimes, it helps to discuss this with another person to gain understanding and insight. It is not necessary to confess these sins to another person, except to get advice and support.

The power of love means to love every single person on earth. There are no boundaries, no restrictions on who should be loved. All people need and deserve love, only because they are creations of the One. Likewise, animals, plants, and all living things are also God's creations. One should always show them the greatest respect and attention. No one should harm animals or misuse plants. Each animal and each plant was created for a specific purpose. Some of these reasons have been lost, but there are people finding the reasons right now. They know there is a reason for the creation of every plant and animal form.

Love is very powerful. If you have love in your heart always, you will live in a state of harmony and peace. If you have feelings of unkindness or think another person is unworthy of your love, you need to examine this thought. You need to see where it came from - do you harbor a false belief? Have you been influenced by someone who does not have love in his heart? Are you thinking that you are better than other people? If so, please examine your beliefs about your own self-worth. I tell you, no matter what your life has been up to this point, God still loves you with unconditional love. You cannot do anything for this to be taken away from you. It always was and always will be.

You see many ill-intentioned people around you, in this world. They have made choices, based on their own unworthy feelings. They do not know the Truth and live a life of falsehoods. God always loves them and invites them back to know a love that is always be there for them. It is true.

It is important that you not judge these people. You may judge an action in your heart, knowing that the action was not based in love. It was based in fear. You can ask that blessings be sent to people who live in fear, making their choices based in fear, and developing a life of falsehoods.

Love leads you into healing. Healing is remembering who you are, who God made you to be. He made you to be a spirit of love. However, you free will gives you the opportunity to turn away from this Truth and live a life of fear. Most of you live in both love and fear, and that requires more energy than what you know. You would have much more light energy, if you made more choices of love, rather than fear. Fear robs you of your human potential.

Please look at your life more closely, now. Live in the present moment, and make choices that are good and right, in the moment. It is much easier to make the right choices, to live in love, if you focus on the now. Many of you make decisions, based on fears about the future. And, these fears never come to pass. You are afraid of what might be, but you neglect to see the good that you have right now. And, you forget to see the good you are.

All of you have lived in a state of pure love and bliss. The dense earth energies made you forget what this state of bliss is. Remember, remember it.

All is well. I leave you with messages of love and hope. I am here to aid you on your life journey, always. I will nudge you along the way, please hear me, listen for me. I am here with you.

All is well. You are loved unconditionally.

Messages from Zadkiel

Message #1 from Zadkiel

I am Zadkiel, known as the Angel of Mercy. Another day, we will talk about mercy, and I will explain what it is. Today, I have another message because it is so important on earth right now. It is something many of you have forgotten how to do. It is very important that you remember to do this, often. Spend some time every day in this activity.

The activity is playing. I think I just surprised you, as you think of the angels as being so serious. Yes, we often have serious messages, and we protect you in times of need. But, playfulness is just as important to you.

When you play, you are reconnecting to that childlike wonder that is still in your soul. This wonder is necessary for you to be able to deal with the harshness of life on earth. It is important to take time out from your busy schedules. We recognize it is becoming more difficult for many of you to have enough money and other resources to live on earth. There are plenty of resources for all but because of greed, some people are taking too much.

Playing is an important form of relaxation. It is good for your bodies, and it is good for your soul. It is easier to feel the joy in your soul. It helps you to relax and become calm. You do not have to pay money to find relaxation. For some people relaxation is just another item on the schedule. Play should be a part of your daily schedule, but do not struggle to find time to play.

When you play, you set aside the worries of your day and your work. Work is also very important, but it is more important to have a balance of work and play. Emphasizing one over the other is not good for you. Find time each and every day to bring some fun and some relaxation into your lives.

When you do this, you will find it much easier to deal with the challenging parts of your life, and the challenges on earth. Play helps you to laugh, and laughter is a special gift to help you get through the difficult times in your life. When you play every day, you do not have to struggle to remember the feelings of play. You had just experienced these feelings yesterday.

I am also known as the Angel of Memory. People call upon me when they are becoming forgetful. Or, they call on me when a parent or loved one is dealing with forgetfulness. This is good.

My main purpose, however, is to help each one of you to remember what your soul state is like. If you spent time each day in play and relaxation, you can reconnect to the lightness and softness of your soul state much easier. It is not easy to do this if your mind and your energy have been focused on the hard parts of your life and on your work.

Playing is a natural part of who you are. Many of you look forward to the few weeks a year you can leave your work and go somewhere else. It is important that you "go somewhere else" each and every day. I am not talking about meditation, or a place of consciousness. I am talking about pure joy. Meditation can take you there too, but too many of you take meditation too seriously. You worry if you are doing it right or wrong. Your mind strays and then you get frustrated. This is counterproductive. It is easier to simply become playful and laugh, and you will find that wonderful peace and harmony within your souls.

Play is not the same for each person, it is individualized. Some people like active play, like dancing or running. Some like to play with animals, or small children. Find whatever it is that you makes you feel like a child again. Remember the most happy of times in your childhood, and that is a clue as to what you can do now. Draw a picture. Fly a kite. Take a deep breath and smile.

You see, I am not such a serious angel after all. We have many characteristics, like you do. And, just like you, we have our special energies and our special tasks in working with you. The Angel of Mercy loves you and reminds you that you are always loved by all of us. Cherish that, like a child is happy to know that Mother and Father love them.

When you remember the love of all of us, the desire to be joyful and playful will come to you naturally. You do not need to put effort into it. Rather, you need to make the space and time for playfulness to manifest in your lives. If you have forgotten how to play, please go to a park and watch the children. They will teach you many lessons. The pure joy on their faces will show you how to find joy. Children are excellent teachers to the adults around them.

Listen to them and watch them. They will help you to remember the feelings you had as a child.

I love you like a parent loves a child, as you are a Child of God. And, we will always love you and guide you and teach you.

Enjoy the rest of this beautiful day.

Message #2 from Zadkiel

Many of you have it backwards. You think your life was predestined to be a difficult one. That is not true. You make the choices and you form the life that you want. You are the creators of your own lives. Please know we want you to have a joyful and happy life. It is possible for all people to live in joy and harmony, but you think your lives are supposed to be difficult and hard. Then, that is exactly what you get.

You have the choice to live a life full of miracles, and of enchantment and joy. You have moments of these, but you think that is all you deserve, a happy moment here and there. That is incorrect thinking. You can live many moments like this, if you would only believe it is possible.

I, Zadkiel, can help you to connect to this beautiful Divine Energy all the time. You can live in peace and harmony, all the time. You do not have to live with little glimpses of it, here and there. That is not part of the Divine plan. But, the Creator has given you free will and the ability to make choices all day long - and, even when you are asleep. Did you know you have a choice about your dreams? You do. You can set the intention before you fall asleep stating what you would like your dreams to be. You can ask for a Divine message. You can ask for guidance for a problem in your life. You can ask for a spirit or a loved one to visit you that night. This is all possible. Believe, and act upon it. You can create whatever you want.

There are so many opportunities for people on earth to grow in love and peace and harmony. Some of you do this already, but very few people take full advantage of this ability. The Divine gave you the ability to create. You can create many wonderful things. Some of you create beautiful buildings and beautiful parks and landscapes. We angels especially love flower gardens, as do our fairy friends. Flowers are a simple and beautiful expression of the beauty you can create on earth. Please give efforts to making beautiful landscapes. It brings good energies to the earth.

Likewise, you can create beautiful landscapes in your lives. These landscapes are your families, your jobs, your relationships. There are many jobs on earth that are not inspiring to you. Sometimes, you stay in those jobs for too long. If your job does not feed your soul, please reconsider. Find something that feeds your soul. It makes all the difference in your lives. You will feel happier and have more energy. You spend many hours on your job, please know that your work should add to your energy, not deplete it. Sometimes, there are not many choices in the area where you live. But, please continue to create work that is pleasing and in harmony with your soul. It is essential that you do so.

Then you must also consider your play time, the time you relax. Some people make this time like a job, and that is not good. Your energy requires times of relaxation and times to become quiet and hear Spirit. There is now more emphasis on this on earth. One of the problems of some religions is that too much time is spent in spoken prayer. The best way to connect to Spirit, to God and to all us beings is through silence. We hear you best, and certainly you can hear us when you are simply quiet. You give us space to talk to you, to communicate with you. This is necessary for your growth and for your connectedness to us.

We hold you in our arms, with much love and peace. We are around you, but many of you are not aware of our presence. We try to get your attention in many ways, but we often feel ignored. Just stop and listen. Look at all the beauty surrounding you. Give gratitude.

We see the turmoil on earth, and we know it is a difficult place to live. All of you chose to be on earth at this time to learn vital lessons for your souls. We see that some of you are becoming aware of this. We applaud and support you. We see some souls who think they are too busy to take out the time to sit in silence. To them, we say: You have it backwards. You must take the time in silence, in order to grow.

Life has become too filled with many unimportant things. There are too many distractions. We ask you to unplug your devices and plug into another whole world. I am referring to the spiritual world. It is an other-world, in the sense the energies are life-giving. Your devices rob you of life. Please consider this mandate.

I know I sound stern, but it is like a parent correcting a child. You are going down the wrong path, and we want to help you to find the path of a happy and fulfilling life. Many of you are going in the wrong direction. Or, you are spending too much time in unimportant activities. There is a balance in everything. You must balance work and play, noise and silence. It is difficult for people, who have physical bodies, to be both busy and silent at the same time. Silence is a special gift from God, so that you can hear the whisperings of Him and of the angels.

Please give us the opportunity to speak with you, all the time. As you grow in living with silence, it will be easier for you to hear our whispers, and feel our nudges towards a certain action or thought. We are here to assist you. It is that simple.

We love you and we want to guide you to a life of peace and harmony. This is where true happiness lies.

Amen.

Message #3 from Zadkiel

There is a new world emerging. It is a world of light and love. Many of you have been preparing for this shift, and it is a major shift on earth. Each person has the opportunity to live in this light, or he can choose to go out with the old-world order. Many problems have been revealed recently in the world. This is so that these things may be released. In some cases, these old problems have been healed. These problems will pass and will no longer exist.

What each person needs to do now is to cleanse themselves of the old ways of being. Jealousies, greed and hatred will no longer exist. It is necessary for each person to be forgiven and embrace mercy. Not forgiving oneself for the sins of the past is not acceptable. This will not allow this person to live in the light. Forgiveness is an essential step.

Forgiveness is available to all. Simply ask, and it shall be granted unto you. Lack of forgiveness keeps you from the Light of the Divine. The Divine has always promised that all you have to do is ask, and you shall receive it. The intention of being forgiven grants forgiveness. There is nothing that the Divine will not forgive. Nothing.

Holding onto past transgressions causes a blockage to God. Why do you clench onto these things that hold you back? God is merciful and He will forgive everything. He loves you unconditionally. Remember this – He loves you unconditionally.

Not accepting this total love is why many of you cannot forgive others – and more importantly, yourselves. You are denying the absolute Love of the Father. Do you understand this? When you think you have committed an act that is so atrocious that God cannot forgive you, you are holding onto a false belief. God always, always forgives, if you believe that He loves you and forgives you.

Do not get caught up in the values of the world. What is important in the world today will not last. It will soon disappear. These words are not said to scare you. Rather, they are being given to you to explain why it is important to become a part of this energetic shift that is already in process. It is nothing to fear. Rather, it is an emergence of what has always been. This world of Light and Love has always been within you, and it has always surrounded you. Only your pre-judgments and false beliefs have kept you from seeing these wonderful ways.

Miracles are all around you, but you do not see them. Love is all around you, but you have only seen a glimpse of God's true love for you. You think you are not worthy of this love. You are mistaken. God made you a worthy, loving and spiritual being. But, you have forgotten this truth.

We angels are here to help you and support you during these turbulent times. Yes, we are working with you all the time. Some of you have become aware of our presence. We are trying many ways to get your attention. There are many distractions on earth today. Please set them aside and commune with us. Nothing would delight us, and the Divine, more. We are here to serve you.

This is a very important message. I am infusing it with Power and Love, so that when you read it you can feel the energies of All that surround you. Please set aside these words for a few minutes. Close your eyes and feel our energies. We are with you, every day, every minute of the day. We ask that you become aware of us and talk to us. Listen and remember who you truly are.

God's mercy and Love is with you. (We have asked Deborah to take few minutes out of typing, so that she can listen with her own heart.)

The work we ask you to do is both internal, and external – as it is with other people and creatures on the earth. Show only kindness and love to others. Every time you do this, people begin to believe they are worthy human beings. We already know their value, but so many people do not see their own value. You can show that to them. They will learn they are beautiful examples of what God has created. Then, they will forgive themselves and they will show love to someone else. The importance of kindness to others cannot be overstated.

Just as we love you, please show love to others. Do not judge and speak only words of kindness. If you hear someone make a judgmental remark, please send that person light and love. You can protect yourselves from the energies of these harsh words, and still send love to the person speaking them. It is obvious that is what is needed in such a situation. Responding with harsh words, or negative thoughts, only expands the negative energies. This is not helpful. Fight hate with love. It is the only way.

Look around you, and you will easily see all the negativity in the world. It is not necessary to turn away from these things. It is better to face them with light and love. That is how negative energies will vanish.

We send you our blessings and our love. You are powerful beings, and you can change the energies in the world. In fact, your intentions and your love is the only way these can be transformed.

Believe this truth. A new world of Light and Love is emerging. Please help to bring it forth.

Blessings to you.

Messages from Ariel

Message #1 from Ariel

I am Ariel, the angel of nature. Nature is healing, as you know. Today, I am talking to you about nature, but most importantly about the healing nature of water. It is therapy for your body and for your soul. Do you know therapy refers to the healing aspects? Therapy comes in many forms, such as talk therapy, physical therapy, and so on. Many of you overlook the many healing aspects of water.

We are working through many people on earth right now to help you understand the healing effects of water. And, there are many sources of healing waters that are especially effective in healing physical maladies. But, all water, that is not contaminated, is good for your body and for your soul. It helps you to go with the flow of life and helps you to deal with all the many difficult parts of life on earth.

Please spend time around bodies of water. These can be the sea, lakes, rivers and creeks, waterfalls, etc. Most places where you live, you are able to visit some kind of body of water.

Let us talk about the mineral spring waters that exist on earth. These are very, very good for you. You should travel to these as much as possible. Then, you need to spend quiet time in the waters and let your body absorb all the wonderful minerals and other energies that exist in the waters. Let me tell you, there are some energies that man is not yet aware of, within these waters. Please trust us when we say – these waters do you much good, more than you know right now. It is important for you to soak your weary bodies in these waters.

If you do not have access to these waters, please buy some of the minerals to put in your baths. Then, take the time to do a good, warm soak in them. This is almost as helpful as sitting in real mineral waters.

There was a time on earth, many centuries ago, that people realized the many health benefits of this kind of therapy. There are now small pockets of understanding, but so much more can be done, with the resources you have on earth, right now.

Some of you study old and ancient ways of healing. This is good. Many of these old ways would be helpful to you now on earth, as these ways are still effective for you. You are depending too much on artificial means. This is not necessary. Everything is available to you through natural means. This is one of God's gifts to you. Every ailment has a way to be healed, through plants, water, food and other means. These ways have been mostly lost and forgotten over the centuries. This does not have to be this way. It is human nature to be greedy, and this greed has forced the natural ways to be lost. You have the capacity to rediscover all of them.

How? All you need to do is to commune with us. We will give you the guidance to find the answers. One problem is that you are too busy with earthly and money concerns. You are not taking the time to sit in quiet and ask for guidance. You are not taking the time to simply be in nature. The more you are quiet, the wiser you become! It is true.

We want to work with you. There are many ways that nature can teach you how to live in community with nature, and with each other. You are creating this strife on earth; it does not need to be this way.

We truly want the best for you, but it seems you are simply too busy to seek the truth. Please, please find time for silent reflection every day. Even better, several times a day. Take time to sit in a forest, walk alone on a path, sit next to a body of water, or sit in the water. Find the peace that is inherently yours. Your life does not have to be a spinning wheel. It can be calm and nourishing and peaceful. It is your choice.

We work with you when you sit in nature and connect with the energies all around you. If you sit quietly, you will feel the energy. It is true.

This is simply the beginning of what is available to you in the outside world. Too many of you spend your entire days and nights indoors. This is stifling to your energetic bodies, and it diminishes your appreciation of the natural world. It makes you disconnected from the remainder of God's creation. This is not the way it needs to be. You can live in harmony with nature, and you will learn to appreciate the many gifts within your outdoor world.

Some of you get outdoors only when you go on an annual trip. How sad. You can connect with nature, and you should connect with nature, at least on a daily basis. Take time to walk, or sit under a tree. It will change your life. It is true.

Gifts surround you, please take the time and make the effort to connect. You will find it easy to connect with the spiritual world, the more you connect with the natural, physical world.

I am a joyful and happy angel, and I want to share these energies with you. It is your birthright to feel joy all the time, every day. Do not put it off, until you are not busy. That time may not come for you. It needs your effort, your choice to live as one with nature.

I look forward to sharing more time with you. I am sincere about this plea. It will change your life on earth, to one of feeling more joy and peace.

Please join me in joyful play in God's garden. I am waiting for you...

Message #2 from Ariel

Because everything is vibration, you can change the energy on earth. Right now, there is much darkness surrounding you. You see many bad things such as racism, sexism, nationalism, and so forth. This can be changed by each of you, as you change your energetic vibrations.

Again, you must spend more time with nature. There is a special power when humans sit with nature. The two energetic vibrations blend together and become more powerful, than just one of you sending energy. One plus one creates a very special energy. You must spend more time in nature, to make this effect.

The darkness is arising now, so that it can be healed. Some of you are suffering from the recent elections, in the US and in other countries. More is to come. It is time for you to change those energies. These can be changed, please believe this. You are more powerful than what you know. You are powerful beings, if you would learn how to use these powers.

Do not underestimate the energies that come from joy and play. This is so important that I may need to repeat myself over and over. That is fine. I will do so, because we care so much about the earth and each one of you. You must learn to play, relax and enjoy life more. These actions will change the energies.

There is much frustration and anger on earth right now. Rather than fight it, change the energy of it. If you respond in anger, that only adds to the negativity energies. You have the choice to respond in love.

What does this mean? Should you love the untruths? No, absolutely not. When you send healing love to these false messages, these messages will lose the negative vibrations. Love always wins, but you must remember to live in love and send love.

I want to bring happiness into your lives. Just slow down and look at the beauty surrounding you. There is nothing more beautiful on earth than nature, unless it has been ruined by humans. Please take time and spend energies on removing some of the toxic places and restore the landscape. Do not let old dilapidated buildings sit. Remove them. Do not let old toxic factories sit, remove them. Continue to work with environmental laws, so that the earth's resources can sustain themselves. These resources are becoming depleted.

There are many people on earth presently who have the right solutions. Some of you are listening to them and becoming more aware. Now, it is time for you to take actions and spread the word among your own communities. This is not an easy task, but a necessary one.

Water will soon be in short supply. It is in endangered presently in some places on earth. Take heed. Learn what you can and start to take actions. What each of you do within your own households will make a difference. However, it will require more actions than these.

Do not listen to men and women of greed. They will try to make false statements and convince you there are no problems at all! This is a lie. There are many problems, and with light and love, and using the gift of your own minds, these problems can be reversed. Speak out against these liars, these greedy people. They are only concerned about their own individual wealth. Some of these people are in powerful positions, and they have believers in their lies. Send all of them light and love. You can win this conflict. You must win this conflict to save the earth.

I cannot tell you how urgent this is. The good news is there is still time for reversal, but it is waning. You must act now. You must support the new ways of saving resources and saving the earth. You must connect with nature, and with us Spirits, to make this work. We want to work with you and continue to guide you in this endeavor.

We feel great joy in every good choice that you make. Even what seems insignificant to you is actually significant. You make a choice in how much water to use when you bathe. Use less, this is a good choice. You choose what to eat several times a day. Think of the environmental impact of each food item you eat.

Also, think about the toxins you eat, and the energy vibration it brings to the world. When you eat processed foods, you continue the chain of artificial and unhealthy toxins. When your body is filled up with toxic materials, the vibrations you emanate out into the world are filled with toxic, negative vibrations. Watch what you consume as this affects the earth.

Good food leads to good health, and people usually accept this theory. They do not yet understand how toxic chemicals in your bodies also affect the earth's vibrations. Please think about this and consume healthy foods. It is both complex and simple.

The toxins on earth are causing many of your illnesses. One purpose is to send a wake-up call to all of you. If the toxins were lessened and eventually disappeared, there would be much less sickness among the peoples. There will still be sickness because there will still be other lessons for your souls to learn. Let me repeat – there will be fewer illnesses. One of the lessons of current diseases is for you to learn the connection between everything. Everything. You do not live in separate houses or communities. You live in one big earth community. There are other communities in the galaxy.

This is difficult for some of you to grasp. As you sit with this information and meditate on it, you will soon realize the layers of Truth within the messages we are giving you.

We are pleased you are taking time to read and contemplate all these messages. We send these to you from our love and concern for you. You are unconditionally loved. If you remembered this, you would take only good actions and not the negative ones.

Many of your leaders do not know this kind of love. They are looking for this love from the masses. They are trying to achieve this, in all the wrong ways. Spreading lies is negative, but they spread these lies so that some people will believe in them. You cannot believe in a false person; you must believe in the Truth. People who live in the knowledge of unconditional love do not need to win your approval. They know the Divine and have complete fulfillment in their lives. Those who seek public office or fame to receive adulation are misguided. Others in public office have the right intentions. Send all of them light and love. Change the negative energies the false leaders put into the world.

I have much to impart today! There is urgency in this message. There is only love from us. Please wrap yourself in the cloak of love and send to the rest of the people on earth. Once they start to see the light and change, they will be grateful. Sending gratitude into the world is better than judgment and hate!

We thank you for your consideration of these serious matters. You can change the earth, and please do so.

We love you.

Message #3 from Ariel

I love you, my children.

There is one thing that is stopping you from feeling peace on earth, and with the earth. The planet itself is suffering from the negative emotions that you have. These emotions are anger and resentment. Many of you are very angry at what is happening on earth. But, you are not seeing the real purpose behind these events. These events are occurring to put light onto them. When bad things are revealed, they can be healed through the light and love you send to them. Do not forget the purpose.

What is needed is forgiveness for those who act out these events, or cause the events to happen. They agreed to play these roles to reveal the wrong's of the world. Some people believe racism no longer exists. This is not true. Racism still exists in many hearts of people, although they may not be comfortable in showing these thoughts to others. When leaders act out on racism, it is in their own hearts, but it is also in the hearts of the people in their nations. It is being shown to all, to be healed.

It is time to forgive. When you carry anger in your hearts, you enable hatred to continue in the world. This anger is no different than what people with racist beliefs feel in their hearts. Please see the similarities and understand when you do not forgive, you also perpetuate these negative sentiments.

We are all mirrors of each other. We angels are sending you the mirror of love, as you are born with love in your hearts. The negative feelings of others can take a hold in your hearts and soon, you become a mirror of them, harboring hate and anger. We know this is not what your heart desires. Your heart desires only love and peace.

Do not be angry towards those who hate and are angry. It is better if you send them love and light. You can change the hearts of others, only after you have changed your own hearts.

This message is vital. Fighting hate with more anger and hate does not work. Only love can turn the hate of others into love. Only love can transform hate into love. First, you must forgive those other people. And you must forgive yourselves for all the negative thoughts and actions you have lived in your own lives.

Forgiveness is the key ingredient in this effort. You must not feel guilty over what you have done in the past. It is over, it is done. You can only change the past by living in love in the present. Yes, past actions can be transmuted and the negative energies can be changed, and healed for the good of all peoples on earth.

Earth is in a precarious position at this time. The healing of the earth must begin in the hearts of human beings. All of you have a spiritual being too, but you often neglect the wisdom of this aspect of yourselves. When you listen to your spiritual self, when you are connected to your spiritual self, you find your own Truth. It takes some quiet time and it takes intention and action. It is simple, and it is difficult, for some of you to achieve. With effort, it is achievable.

We help you when you set the intention to find peace in your lives. We work with you and we guide you. We send you thoughts and little nudges to help you on your path. We are always there for you, even when you do not recognize us or ask us for our help.

When hearts change, the world changes. Love in your hearts will spread out to love everywhere in the world. Many problems would disappear, such as hunger, droughts, wars, and other environmental issues. You would return to earth being a paradise for all peoples. Paradise - your soul remembers this time on earth. It is such a beautiful thing to see all of nature and humans living in total harmony. It can be achieved again. Much work needs to happen first.

We will guide you along the way. We are at the ready. Take time to breathe and to connect with us and with your Divine Source. Slow down and smell the roses, as they say. There is great wisdom in this statement. You are too rushed, and you rush to judgment too quickly about other people.

Remember your pure heart in its earliest days. When you were babies, you had only love in your hearts. You were trained to think differently as the years went by. You saw others judge, and you learned to judge. You saw others become angry and hateful, and then you learned to be angry and hateful. This is not your heart's, nor your soul's, desire. Your heart only wants to love.

Find that place within your hearts again. Forgive those who have hurt you and hated you. Forgive, forgive,

forgive. Your heart will then be open to receiving Divine love and giving only Divine love to others.

You are children of God. Children of God know love and peace. War and hatred must end on earth. This is the time for you to bring these beautiful feelings to earth. Then, peace will be possible again.

We embrace you with love and light.

Messages

from

Uriel

Message #1 from Uriel

My children, I have come to you today to talk about the importance of study. Yes, I am sometimes known as the intellectual angel. All of you have been blessed with a high intellect, but many of you are not utilizing it to the fullest degree. I am here to help you return to the art of studying. It is a blessing for you, and you will grow in many ways through this art.

Study means that you will read, listen and acquire new knowledge. In your modern world, there is much information available to you. In past ages, acquiring a book was very difficult. Today, there are many, many affordable books. You can access these through your libraries and your internet and your bookstores.

Then, you must sit down with these books and spend much time with them. It is time to turn off your internet and your televisions and pay attention to the knowledge and wisdom held between the covers of a cherished book. I will assist you in finding the right book for you, where you are on your path of learning.

Your intellect hungers for eternal knowledge. Feed your intellect and your life will change. You will learn Truths and you will see how these Truths exist in your lives. When you learn, you will become more connected to this Eternal Wisdom. Your lives will be very blessed.

You can continue your jobs and your busy lives. All we ask is that you spend a little time every day, with learning. This will help to refresh you and fill your heart with love. You will realize your role in bringing peace and love to the world. You will learn what your heart's desire is.

Some of you (like Deborah) have learned that you will be guided to a certain book. Deborah remembers a day when she wanted a spiritual book at the library. One title popped out at her, but she continued to walk past it. But, we told her to turn around and pick up the book. She felt the urge to turn around and she did. The title did not reflect what was in the book, but she got it anyways. The book was very meaningful to her. We guided her to this book as it is what she needed at that time on her path. We will do the same for you. You only need to listen and follow our hints.

Study is very important. For those of you who have a Bible, or a book from your religion, please spend time with these books. Be open to the messages held within the words. Many of these books have a message on the surface, but there are also many hidden messages, under the surface. If you ask for all the meanings of certain phrases, or sections, these will be revealed to you. You must have an open mind and heart. You will soon understand why these books are so rich with meaning for you. Do not take time with these books lightly. These are important tomes in your world.

There are many other books that are rich with meaning and important to your spiritual growth. Some seem heavy to you, and others will seem light, almost fun. Some of these fun books may be a memoir of someone's path, or a funny story. These stories will be enriching to you.

Let me talk about your internet. There is some good material on the internet, but please be careful. There is also misleading or incorrect information on the internet.

What you need to do is ask for spiritual guidance if you want to read from the internet. We will guide you to correct understandings of the Truth.

Also, there are teachers of Truth and teachers who have incorrect information. We will guide you through your gift of discernment to listen to Truth and to turn away from falsehoods. Without guidance, this can be difficult for you to discern on your own. This is because many false people know how to dress up the information to make it look whole and right. It is not whole and right; it is false. We will guide you when you find this information. Be open to our words, these will appear as thoughts in your mind.

Study is a beautiful time, and some of you have already found the pure joy of learning new Truths. Sometimes, you already know the Truth but you have forgotten it. Or, you hear it in a new way that makes it more understandable to you.

As the angel of intellect, let me reiterate the importance of this gift from God. Only people, human beings, were bestowed this wonderful gift. God chose to give this to you so that you can find your way Home to eternity. Use this gift well.

For those of you who have chosen a lifetime of study, we say this is your soul purpose, and you are bringing this gift to earth. Not all people have study as a life purpose, but all people need to take some time out of their life's work to do some study and reading. Some of you will be called to teach reading to those who have not had the opportunity to learn to read. Let us say – this is a very, very important task. We are very pleased with those who teach others to read, whether it is to an adult who never learned, or to a child of yours. Teaching someone to read, and teaching them to love to read, is a beautiful gift. Parents, always show your children your appreciation for books and learning. In today's world, children often set aside books for electronic toys. Limit time with electronics and show them the richness of the printed word.

We helped to bring the printed word into the world. Inventors and people who made progress in your world listened to our whisperings. You too receive whisperings. When you take time to listen to them, wonderful things will happen.

Also, listen to the times you hear the same message more than once. If you hear about a book more than once, it is our urgings that you find a copy and read it! There is something in the book for your mind to learn. Sometimes, we may lead you to an internet site or talk that will be important for your spiritual growth and your understanding of a Truth.

We will continue this conversation another time. Please heed these words and find a time for study. It is vitally important.

Message #2 from Uriel

People see me as a serious angel and in many ways, I am. I take the knowledge of God very seriously, and I work hard to impart this among your peoples. This knowledge is very important for the highest good of mankind.

I am also an angel of fun and playfulness. Just like you, I need to have balance in my life as an angel. People on earth have many responsibilities and often they do not take time for fun and play. Let me remind you, fun and play are very important to you. This time of relaxation brings energies into your lives that you think are not that important. They are very important in keeping your energy fields balanced and healthy.

On earth, there are many diseases and illnesses. Yes, fun and play would decrease these illnesses more than what you realize. The stress levels that you maintain invite these diseases into your body fields of energy. Your bodies are open to these invasive viruses. This is an important lesson for you to learn. If you are relaxed, you would not be susceptible to these diseases. Your body would fight them off, and you would not suffer in the many ways that you suffer now.

There is too much dependence on artificial chemicals and substances. Returning to the natural order would be beneficial to you in various ways. God made the earth to be healthy and to be nurturing to you. But your actions have placed a cloud over the natural order. In some areas of the world, these clouds are visible to you. In other areas, they may not be visible but they still exist. The choices people on earth have made created this unhealthy environment. Then, your actions add to this state of unhealthy living. The stress and responsibilities you take on all the time add yet another level to this sad state of affairs.

All of you have been blessed with intelligence. You must learn to listen to this intelligence and cultivate this intelligence to fully understand the harm you bring to the planet and to your physical bodies. Continuing on your high levels of stress will only add to your imbalance in all living things.

Please take the time to enjoy life, and relax. We know about the phrase, "stop and smell the roses." There is great wisdom within this phrase. First, you must stop the merry-go-rounds of life that you have created. Then, you must use your God-given senses to understand and relish the natural world where you live. Smell is a beautiful gift of God. Do you fully appreciate it?

When you smell a rose, you become aware of the miracle of life that God has bestowed upon you. The rose is delicate and strong, smells heavenly, and it is beautiful beyond words. It is a symbol of love. You think of the romantic kind of love. Its first symbolism is God sending you love, each moment of your lives. The rose is an eternal sign of God's love for you.

If God loves you, then you must take the utmost care of your bodies, your souls, and the planet earth. It is not too late to do this. There is still time for you to save the earth. Please start now.

Begin with your own bodies. The more you relax, the more you will be able to receive directions on what you must do. Each person is called to bring healing to the earth, and each of you has a specific role. This is true.

Let me say it again – each of you has a specific role, a purpose, in saving the earth. There are generations after you who want to come and live on earth. They want to play and frolic in this beautiful nature that surrounds you.

There are forces who are ignoring the earth, and some of these forces have great power right now on earth. This is happening because people are choosing the wrong priorities, out of greed and individual goals. Please remember everyone, and everything, is connected. When you make self-centered decisions, the ramifications can be severe for other people – and for you. This is true.

Our love for you is never-ending. Ask for guidance in what you can do to bring harmony and peace back to the Planet Earth. When you ask, you will hear the answer. The answer will be given, with complete love and confidence that you are able to carry it out. No one is given a task that is impossible. All guidance given to you is possible, in practical terms.

I have allowed my intelligence to take over! When you hear what your task is, it will become a major goal in your life. But again, it must be balanced with fun and playfulness. The balance is a necessary ingredient in accomplishing all good things.

We are here to guide you, and to serve you. We are the messengers of God. We love you and we only wish for all good and beautiful happenings in your lives.

Blessings to you today, and every day of your lives.

Message #3 from Uriel

Dearest One,

This is a time of great spiritual growth for you. You have chosen this book from your desire to become more closely connected to the Divine. You are searching and reading, and praying and meditating. These things are important to you as you greatly desire the closeness your soul has already experienced in previous life times. This is indeed a very special time for you.

Sometimes, you feel fear as you do not know where this path will lead you. Be not afraid, as God has a plan for you and for your life. Trust the process of growth. It will only bring growth to your understanding and knowledge.

You need not fear any changes you will make in your life. All these changes are for the highest good, even when it seems there is no good coming from the changes. Yes, relationships may change but that means it was time for those relationships to end. These were not contributing to your spiritual well-being.

You may also decide to change jobs or your career path. Again, let me assure you these changes are necessary for your spiritual growth. There are many jobs on earth that are not fulfilling and do not contribute to spiritual understanding. There are jobs that you must endure for the sake of your soul's growth and for you to learn your soul's life lessons. Once these lessons have been learned, the job can be released. You can move forward in your life. These challenges are placed in your life for a purpose. Once the purpose is fulfilled, the challenges will be lifted from your path.

The time is now on earth for great transitions in spiritual understanding. Many, many changes are occurring. Old systems and hierarchies are disappearing, and a new world order will happen. This new world order will not look like the one that has existed for centuries. There will be a sense of oneness with all other human beings. Nationalism and other false structures will disappear. This is good. It is necessary for all to understand the true nature of being One with each other - and being One with the Divine and all spiritual beings. There are no divisions, all these divisional structures are false. They have served a purpose, however. They have taught you the many problems with this kind of limited thinking. All the wars, poverty and destruction of the earth's resources were born from these divisions. A new world order is on the way.

Likewise, some of the worst leaders you have ever seen have recently come into power. This is to demonstrate how embracing the wrong values only leads to great problems on earth. You are also seeing how many people still believe in these old ways. Please send prayers and energy for all these people to heal these old belief systems. Some people will not be able to make this choice, and many will be leaving the earth plane soon.

Please send love and healing thoughts to those wrong-thinking leaders and ask for ways to take away their power on earth. This is done through love, not fear. Love your enemy; that is always paramount in assisting change in other people. And, love yourselves. Only love, not fear-based thoughts and actions, can manifest good changes on earth.

You are living in times of major transitions. You may feel tired and discouraged at times. Or, you may feel hopeless and disempowered. Nothing is further from the truth. It is only through empowerment, fueled by thoughts of love, that result in everlasting change. You chose to live during such a difficult time period, as your soul was committed to these necessary earth changes. You may be familiar with the term lightworker. It simply means you came to earth to bring light to fight the dark forces. We honor you for your courage and your strength. Living on earth now is one of the greatest tasks ever available for souls.

The best armor you have for the battles ahead is your spiritual awareness and consciousness. This is not a war of killing others or using destructive weapons. It is a war of fighting energies. Which energy will win? The one of love and peace, not the one of destructive power and greed. We know the outcome. Armor yourself with God's love and strength. With the right intentions, love will win, at the end of this era.

We hold you in the palm of our hands. We surround you with light and love. There is nothing to fear. The more you live in spiritual graces, the more protected you are. All you need do is ask for protection, and it is there. This war is not about living longer on earth, it is about the earth living longer! You will be able to save the planet, and most of humankind, with your spiritual strength. Love will win. Yes, love will win.

How long this war will last is totally dependent upon the people on earth. The greater the numbers of people who will send this light, the quicker it will end. The time is approaching….please be prepared.

There are many resources available to you in your modern world. Read, meditate, pray and be with others like you. Continue on your path of growth. Become more sensitive to all the energies on earth. This will give you even more incentive and purpose as you journey through these times.

I send you my love and my support, as do all the other angels here on the heavenly plane. We are watching and we are giving you signs and ways to enrich your growth. We are very pleased and excited about the thousands and thousands of people who are waking up and growing right now, in the ways of connecting to us and to the Supreme Being.

I must leave now, but I am always with you. I will continue to disperse information and support, when the time is right for each of you. We have the ability to work with many individuals at the same time. Tine is not the same in the heavens, as it is on earth. It is not linear. Do not worry about this, but know we are always with you.

In great love and appreciation of your efforts,
Uriel

Messages from Gabriel and Michael (alternatively)*

*From Deborah – These messages were presented to me in this format, with Gabriel and Michael "taking turns" to present messages of peace and harmony.

Message #1 from Gabriel

I am the angel of communication. And, I am the angel of other things but we will discuss them another day. Today, we focus on communication, especially communication from you to us. One of the best ways for you to communicate is to speak an intention. An intention is a statement of what you want to achieve, or something you want in your lives. It is like setting a goal and saying it out loud.

When you state an intention, it is a message to us. Often, you think of messages only coming from us to you. But, you can send us messages too.

When you make a strong statement of a desire, and you infuse it with love and power, we will hear it. If it is for the highest good, it will happen. We will help you to make it happen – that is what we do, we give you assistance every time you ask.

Strong intentions have a power unto themselves. It is making an idea real, and making it possible. If you state the intention "I will write a book", it will happen.

Again, we will use Deborah as an example. We know Deborah loves books. She always has been a great reader. We watched her when she was a little girl reading in the bedroom she shared with her sisters. She went on many adventures through her books. In the back of her mind, she said she would like to write a book. She even sat down at the typewriter a few times, but no good ideas came to her. That is because the time was not yet ready for her book. Many things had to happen in her life, and she needed a greater understanding of spiritual life before this book was ready to be born. When the time was right, the book flowed.

It is the same with this book. She was not ready, and the readers of this book, were not ready for these messages. People are ready now. People are looking for guidance – and more importantly, for the Truth. Many other ways of us communicating Truths to you are occurring right now, on earth.

As you know, communication happens both ways. Sometimes, we communicate with you, and sometimes you communicate to us. There must be a speaker and listener. Then, the roles are reversed.

To be a good communicator, you must find your authentic voice. This happens when you live in your authentic truth. Each of you has the ability and wisdom within to discover who you really are. Yes, we will help you, but the self-discovery is for you to make. You are so precious and so loved. You will know, and speak about this, when the truth has been discovered within your hearts. Your true voice will be able to speak out, and you will help others to find their own truth. It is vitally important that you discover the wisdom within, and that you share this wisdom with others. When you do this, it will become easier and easier for people to live in harmony and peace.

There are many falsehoods in your world today. No matter the subject, there will be untruths spoken by some people. We are not here to judge those people. It is better for you to walk away and live in your own true beliefs. Avoid conflict whenever possible. There will be times when you need to speak Truth, and dispute untruths, but do not insult the other person.

You have had many leaders who have done just that. Usually, they are not political leaders but leaders of Truth. Jesus was able to model this behavior for you. He turned the other cheek. He did not argue with others, but simply spoke Truth as he knew and understood it. This is the human side of Jesus, and it is attainable for any one of you. You can also live and speak of Truth in a nonconflictual way.

We know that may seem difficult, but know it is always possible. If you tell us you need help or guidance in a specific situation, we will always be there to give you a path, a way, of expressing yourself. It will be for the highest good.

Sometimes, when you express a desire or intention to us, it is filled with anxiety or fear. It is not an intention of pure thought. The intention is fear-based. When an intention is infused with fear, rather than love, we are hesitant to respond. We can see the bigger picture and we know it may soon go awry. The emotion of fear can overtake the emotion of love, and it will not be successful.

You may not ask for something because you do not think you are good enough to attain the goals you truly desire. You do not think you are worthy of such an achievement. This is false thinking, and we will not be able to give your intention our full power.

In order for an intention to work it must be in alignment with our energies. We never work from fear, but always from love. When you set an intention with love, it aligns with our energies. It will be for the highest good of you and other people around you. It will succeed.

At this present moment, many intentions we hear are full of distress and worry. It is like hearing loud static when you turn on your radios. The intention is not clear to us, and the words feel confused and undecipherable. We are unable to put our energies into the effort. In fact, we decide not to do so, as these actions may deplete our own power and misguide you in the future.

We are here to help and assist you. We know life is especially difficult on earth right now. There are many negative energies, because there are many greedy and misguided people on earth. Too many are being self-centered and they do not care what happens to others. You, however, do care about others and manifesting peace on earth.

Let me say this – peace on earth is achievable. Each of you needs to do your own part in establishing this peace. More and more of you will work together, and it will be manifested.

Listen to the intentions borne from your heart. Take times of quiet to hear the whisperings that exist within you.

Dwell on these whisperings, as these will expand. These will be verbalized as intentions, whether spoken in silence or out loud. When these intentions, born out of love and harmony, come our way, we will respond. We will respond with great love and great power.

The intentions will then become real on earth.

We honor you for your efforts in living in alignment with us. It is the only way earth will be healed. Let us always find a way to speak and listen to each other.

Peace be with you always!

Message #1 from Michael

Today we will be talking about Divine Timing. Right now, today, there are many protests going on throughout the world. This is very good. These are the good energies fighting against the negative energies of the world. Many things had to happen to stir up the emotions of people who have the right understanding of the divinity of human beings, of their spirits. Too many people were still stuck in the old paradigm that some people are better than others. This is totally a false understanding. All human beings have been created in the image of God. This does not mean that

God looks like a human being. What it refers to is that each person has the same energy, the soul, and God, has.

It is the same energy that we angels have too. It is all the same. This Divine Spark and wisdom each person has can be enlarged. The person will have the wisdom and insight shared by God and other spiritual beings. Or, the spark within can be left to die. When it is nearly extinguished, the person can turn to evil things. Or, the person can live a life without direction or hope. There are many human beings on earth where the spark is diminished. There is still hope that these people will learn about God and the spark will grow. It is your job to find those lost souls and help them to become reconnected to their true selves, and to God and other spiritual beings.

Today is the day of the Women's Marches all over the world. People are speaking out about human rights. They see the interconnectedness between all human beings. They understand there is just one family, and everyone on earth is connected. If one person is treated unjustly, it affects the energies of the whole, of the earth and all its people.

I came through today because it is a day of power. The power lies within, and it does not lie within any one government or any one human leader. Some leaders think they are better and more important than other people. This is not true.

Each person has the power within to live a life of integrity and goodness. Even those who may not know they are a part of the Divine Energy, they may know there is something greater than themselves. They do not have the words to describe what they feel. It has been this way since the beginning of time. Centuries ago, it was easier to see the greatness of the All, through nature. The big cities and the multitudes of people on earth make it more difficult to see. But many still see and know the Divine.

I am here to help each one of you to find the power within, the power that is connected to your soul, to your own divine nature. When this connection is made by each person, then the earth will be healed.

Let me clarify – not every individual will seek this power and this knowledge. When the majority of people do, they will be able to turn the tide of aggressiveness and greed. What is needed is a majority of Divine power to win out over the forces of evil and indifferent energies.

The indifferent energies are a problem. Indifference promotes a stagnation of strong, good energies. While these evil forces have been rising, many people have awakened. They no longer live in indifference. They understand it is time to get up and fight. The fighting is not what you think of as conflicts and war. The battle is won through the Divine Light. As more and more people understand this phenomenon and live in light, and expand light, the dark forces will be overcome. They will leave the earth.

Divine Timing dictated that in order for the light to win out, the evils that still existed on earth had to be exposed. Leaders who were racist and misogynists were allowed to be in power; the people who still had these beliefs in their hearts placed them in power. I am not talking about only one leader, but many leaders who are in power in today's world. Masses of people have become self-centered and cared only for their own welfare, or perhaps the welfare of others in their countries. They did not care about people from other countries, cultures or religions.

This is wrong. Let me repeat, all persons have the Divine Spark within them. All persons have a soul and a spirit. Each person is unconditionally loved by God. All your Scriptures say this; yet, people who follow specific religions often think their religion is the only right one. Whenever this belief is embraced, it is stating other people's religions are false. That is not true.

We honor you and bless you.

Message #2 from Gabriel

Oh, my little weary ones. I see how distressed you are becoming with all the world events. Please know these too shall pass, as each of you finds a way to peacefully protest actions taken by your leaders. Do not be weary. You are fighting a good fight. Do it in peace and love. All is well.

I bring you glad tiding of joy and celebration today. Celebration, you say. How can we celebrate with these problems in the world, you ask? These problems are arising for eternal healing. Now is the time for you to bring in light and love, and these will be gone. This is the reason for celebration. With the gift of free will, you can find the power of light and love within you. It has always been on the earth. Sometimes, it has been permitted to shine strongly – through love-filled decisions that people made at that time. Now, you have the same opportunity. You can expand the love and light. Celebrate.

Gently, gently, please take a deep breath, right now. When you feel yourselves becoming distressed, do not live in that energy. Rather, stop and take a deep breath. You will fill your physical body with life-giving energies. You will be able to emanate this energy from your body and bring healing to all negative situations.

It is essential you understand how this works, so that you can activate this any time you are faced with negative energies. It is most simple. Stop and take a deep breath. Bring in the life-giving forces that is Divinely yours to have. You do this automatically, all the time. You breathe without setting the intention to breathe.

When you breathe with intention, the synergy of your intention, along with the love of the Divine, you create strong, authentic power. Everything is possible. There are no limitations.

When you become upset with negative actions by others, your mind has already placed limitations on the circumstances. You do not see how it can be fixed, as it seems impossible to do so. It may seem too many people are against love, or people with earth-given powers (vs God-given powers that each of you already possess) will have all the say. This is not true. Intentional power is most effective, very effective.

I, Gabriel, always bring into your beings strong, yet gentle, energies. Approaching these difficulties with gentleness and gratitude are more powerful than manmade powers. You see, political leaders, corporate leaders, and the like are truly illusions. They have gained their power through manmade structures, and all these structures are temporary. They can fall away. Your authentic power cannot be taken away from you, ever.

That being said, many of you do not understand this and do not grow, or exercise, this power within you. Some of you are not aware of your power. Or, you think this power was not realized by your parents, or other people in this manmade authority.

The truth is when you are faced with power struggles on the earth, it is from this flimsy manmade structures. Your corporations will go away some day and even your nationalistic structures will disappear. The realization that all people are One, and all things that happen affect all other people, will be realized. The earth will be very different than it is right ow.

Imagine what this earth will look like! Imagine all the peace and harmony when countries quit trying to overtake other ones. Imagine being surrounded by the love of all people. This is cause for celebration! This will happen.

Your job is to discern what you are being called to do – right now, in the present moment. It is good to know the history of your country and your people, but do not live in this information. Live in the present moment. That is what each of you can count on. The present moment, the now. What can you do right now? How can you live in love and light – right now?

Imagine there is a large group of celestial beings ready to assist you in these endeavors. This large group is here NOW. Each one of us wants to assist you in these essential efforts. We hold you in peace. We honor you. We love you.

The earth has gone through many transitions over the millenniums. It is true. Another transformation is occurring in the present times. We hold you gently through these difficulties. We assist you in your part in creating this transformation.

As each of you transforms individually, these energies are then anchored into the earth's energy fields. Each time you have a positive thought or deliberately send energy out onto your earth and its people, then change is taking place. It is very simple for you to do.

Right now, think a happy thought of celebration. Then, make a statement of gratitude. Send love to someone whom you cherish. Feel the energy in your body. Isn't it wonderful? Notice your breathing. Isn't it deep and luxurious? This is living in peace and harmony. These few moments have assisted in the earth's transformation. Please acknowledge that you have this power. You do.

Imagine the happiest celebration you could ever have. Think of the smiles, the joy in your heart, the good feelings in your soul. Celebration brings these energies into the earth, and your intentional response to these energies will anchor them and heal the earth and its people.

We hold you in our arms. Always ask for our help. We are always there to love you, support you and guide you - all the time.

My love to each of you.

Message #2 from Michael

Today, we will discuss the power of integrity. Integrity means being true to yourself. It means being authentic, or not being inauthentic. Many people do not live within their own integrity. They are trying to please other people, or act in ways that other people expect. This is not living in truth and integrity.

When a person lives in integrity, they are always the same person no matter the setting, no matter with whom they are. Because they live in accordance with their souls, they find an inner peace that is truly awesome. They no longer play games with other people, and more importantly, with themselves. This game-playing takes too much energy away from your souls. It requires you to always be on stage, like an actor. In fact, you are an actor. You are acting like another person; someone you think will be more acceptable to others.

When you live this way, you pay a large price. In your own hearts, you know this is wrong. You know it is not sustainable. In fact, you take breaks from acting this way. You look forward to time away, whether is time away from your jobs, your relationships, or the acting you are doing. When you live in accordance with your soul, it actually requires much less energy. It is natural, it is good. It is what God wants for you. It is what your own Divinity knows, it is the right place to be.

There are times when you live your life purpose, and you know how good it feels. There is a harmonious energy that emanates from your soul and your body. Even if you do not recognize it, please listen to others' comments. They will say something such as - you seem happy right now, or you seem to be at peace. There are times when we whisper these words to others, to speak out loud to you. These are affirmations that you are walking the correct path.

Often, when people think of power, they are talking about the power you have with other people. True power lies within you. You do not have to be a leader, in the world's sense, to be a leader within your own heart and soul. The world would be a better place if the leaders lived in their own hearts and souls first, and allow this knowingness, this wisdom, to guide them. There are some leaders in today's world who do this. Most do not.

Each of you has a sphere of people around you. You can be a leader in your own sphere. This is different than the world's understanding of leadership. In this sense, we are talking about being a model. Each of you can find someone in your lives, right now, whom you look up to. What is it about this person that makes you want to be like them? It is simple. This person lives in truth and integrity. The truth is within, and they have used their free will to live in a way that matches this wisdom.

All of you do this some of the time, at least. Use your free will, to live there more moments of every day. You know the feeling of resonance, when you have paid attention to your wisdom and make good choices for yourself. You sense the flow in your lives when you become aware of these whisperings and make decisions that respond accordingly.

This is a time of great transition on the earth. The new age is here. There are many more choices for you to make. Life is not as simple as it once was. Because of these complexities, which man has created, there are so many more choices to be made. This is good. Civilization is advancing. You have chosen a wonderful time to live on earth. You have created this reality, this illusion, so that your souls may advance.

The mission is twofold. One part of the mission is to take responsibility for your own individual soul and its growth. Free will, and knowledge and prayer, will assist you in achieving this goal.

The second part of the mission is to bring love and peace into the earth. This is for Mother Earth. She has willingly allowed herself to be used in such a way that she is now an endangered species. People need to act now to prevent this from happening. It is not too late. Every moment of every day, you have choices. You can honor the natural resources she has provided for your use. But, you must also take actions to replenish these resources. You must determine what is necessary to not only stop the carnage, but also to heal the earth. Each person has a role in this healing. Each person has the free will to continue as is, or to change the course of events.

So, not only must each person make decisions to heal Mother Earth, but each person must make choices to become a model for others. If you change your habits and become more aware, you model this for other people. They will learn from you. One person may be focused on water supply, while another is focused on global warming. While these are connected, the emphasis is different. Each person has a role to play. As each person makes individual, small decisions, the energy shifts. You absorb the energy from others, and others absorb the energy from you. The entire course has changed. This is necessary.

Living in truth and integrity applies to each individual's life. It applies to each individual's soul. But, it also applies to every other person. The truth is there is only One. This One includes all spirits, all human beings, the consciousness. It includes anything and everything you can imagine. The Ascended Masters work with you closely, as they have had the experience of life on earth.

Please call upon any of us, at any time. We too are invested in your spiritual growth, and to the benefit of the Whole. We are One, with you.

We honor you and we support you. Ask and you shall receive. With you is the Power of the One. Listen and take action. Simply ask for our help.

Yes, I am known as the Archangel of Authentic Power, the Archangel of Truth. Let me remind you that all angels, and all spirits in our realm who are working to give you guidance, are available. You simply need to ask.

We will infuse you with Power that you have barely tapped into, at this point in the earth's history. It is much stronger and more powerful than you realize. Please ask us for guidance and support. We are here to help you every minute of every day.

Amen.

Message #3 from Gabriel

As you know, I am often drawn with a trumpet, an instrument that I am blowing into, and making beautiful music. It is a sign of my work as a messenger. There is another message within these drawings, a message that is sometimes forgotten.

The message is that music can heal your souls. Sound can bring physical healing to your physical bodies. Music has always been a part of the energy on earth. The understanding of how music influences people has waxed and waned.

Music is all around in today's world. The healing powers of music are often ignored. Let us examine this a bit further today.

Within sound, there are energetic vibrations that reverberate into the atmosphere. There is beautiful, soul-enriching music around you. Many people do not spend time with this kind of music. They would rather listen to the harsh, ear-splitting varieties. These songs also send out vibrations to the world. Unfortunately, these vibrations do not add to the harmonious sounds that can be created. They detract from these sounds and their vibrations.

Choose your music carefully. Search for the soul-soothing music. Those sounds will bring peace and harmony into your lives, and into the world. Sound is a very powerful anecdote to the ills on the earth, both individually and collectively.

It has been reported from those who have near-death experiences that they heard music unlike music they have ever heard before. This is partially true. They have heard this music before, before they incarnated on earth. They do not remember it though. That part of the brain was turned off. If you remembered what it was like on the other side, you would pray to be relieved from the heavy energies on the earth! You came back to earth to learn life's lessons and to help other people. Experiencing the glories of the other side, before your transition time, would not be a wise thing to do!

When people hear just a bit of the heavenly sounds, they yearn for that kind of awesome beauty. You do get small glimpses of it, through some of the most beautiful songs on earth. Some of your great composers, like Beethoven and Mozart, have come relatively close to the sounds in heaven. But, when played against some of the negative energies that exist on earth – due to the free will of its citizens - the sounds are denser than those on a higher plane of existence.

The more you play, or listen to, these lovely pieces, the more vibrations of love and harmony you can bring to your souls, and to the earth. Whenever you have some free time, or you are simply working in your homes, play a lovely piece of music. As you do this more frequently, you will feel the lightness enter your hearts and your physical bodies. You will raise the vibrations in your homes to a new level. When others enter your homes, they will feel a difference, although they will not be able to identify the source.

The images of me playing a trumpet is simply to remind you of this beautiful gift. There are other sounds you can make, besides music, that can also raise the vibrations. Chanting, humming, drumming and other instruments - all raise the vibrational level. Some instruments are associated with certain cultures. That instrument met a vibrational need within that culture, and we gave assistance to bringing forth the image of the instrument within the minds of creative people. These people were open, although perhaps not totally aware, of what they were developing. The ancient tribes who brought forth drums needed that kind of instrument to create order and peace within their own groups. The same thing occurred with string instruments, keyed instruments and so forth. The inspirational thought within those creators' minds were whisperings from us. We could see what vibrations were needed, and we gave this gift to those people.

You live in a world with many, many choices to follow. Ask for guidance as to what kind of sound would be most helpful to you individually, and to your culture and the world as a whole. Simple music, simple chants would make a difference now. Music is a reminder of living in the present moment. Each note lasts just a moment.

We ask you now to put down this book, after you read these instructions:

Think of a moment when a musical piece totally touched you. You were taken by surprise. You felt a closeness with God and the heavens, unlike any you have felt before. You were stopped in your tracks. Something resonated with your heart and your soul. You have never forgotten this moment. Sit with this memory. Feel the energy you felt within you. Savor this energy. Ask this energy to expand within your heart and you soul.

After a few minutes, come back to this book.

Each of you will have a different memory. This memory touched you individually, because it was something your soul needed at that moment in time. Your soul also needed to sit with that memory, and the energy it produced. Re-experiencing it now also indicates your soul was replenished with this energy – in the present moment.

Cherish the gift of music and of sound. It is a blessed way to connect with us and it is a blessed way to bring needed energies for peace and love into your being, and into the world.

When you ask for assistance in this arena, it will be given to you. Listen to our words, listen to our whisperings and your inner urgings. These are all gifts for your growth. These are all blessings.

We are always here to assist you, in any way necessary for your growth.

Message #3 from Michael

We protect the children. You too are being asked to pay special attention to children at the present time. Many children have come to earth to teach you many lessons. We are protecting them on this mission.

The refugee children are a special group of children who have chosen especially difficult circumstances. They are here to awaken all the people to their plight. This plight is also real for their parents and other family members. They have chosen this special sacrifice, of living in harsh conditions and looking for daily food, to awaken all peoples. The new fighters on earth have no compassion for these children. Therefore, you are being called to have extra compassion for them, to help balance compassion needed for all children.

Let me repeat – these children have chosen this difficult path to help each of you to grow in compassion for all peoples. Right now, there is a shortage of compassion for earth's people, who do not look like you, talk like you, or think like you. Diversity is part of God's plan to help you wake up and see that all people are unconditionally loved.

There are people in leadership who display this attitude of "I am better than you." And, these leaders have many followers. Other people, however, see the falsehood in this statement (although at times, those same thoughts have crossed their own minds).

All of you are being called to form a new world order. This world order is one of equality for all. It is one of basic human rights for all. It is one of unconditional love for all. All people are called to make life honorable on earth. Too many lives are destroyed for the selfish attitudes of some people.

Each person on earth can have a self-centered attitude. Some are subtle and some are very clear. Most of you reading these messages have had subtle self-centered thoughts. When you waste natural resources without much thought, you have lived a self-centered ideology. If you become more mindful of natural resources, for example, then you are thinking of the whole, of all peoples. If you waste water, then you have taken water away from someone who is thirsty. If you waste wood, you have taken away warmth from someone. Please look at your own motivations and your own beliefs, so that the world is still vibrant for the next generations of children.

Our protection of children goes beyond just earthly needs. At the present moment, there are special children who have come in to spread spiritual knowledge and Truth. They are small lightworkers. When a child says something amazing, beyond their years in a worldly sense, please take notice. This wisdom came from deep within their souls. The time was right for this statement, as this statement was made to help you grow in a spiritual sense. These children are amazing, please take notice and grow in awareness.

My protection is for all people who ask. I will protect you physically, emotionally and spiritually. If someone throws an insult at you that is hurtful, ask for my protection. I will fight off the energies that came from that insult - so that you will not hold onto it and develop a new emotional block. The enlightened children are doing this naturally. When other children throw insults at them, due to their wisdom, these insults will not reach their emotional bodies of energy. I will slash the energies before they reach the children's bodies. I will do the same for you, please ask for this kind of protection.

It is no accident that I am illustrated as the angel with a sword. You may visualize me slashing away at harmful negative energies that are being sent to you, by others' words and thoughts. I will slash them so that there is no effect upon your being. This is my role.

If you are in harm's way, and it is not your time to leave the earth, or it is not to your benefit to have this injury or illness, I will protect you from this. There are always opportunities for your body to become injured or ill. You can ask for my protection, to not experience these problems.

Some of you, however, made an agreement before this lifetime to experience these difficulties. This may have been due to your own need for soul growth, or you may have chosen to help others who are affected by your personal difficulties. Or, it may be for both reasons. If it is meant to be, I will not protect from the agreed-upon diagnosis, but I will protect you in other ways. I can give you solace and calmness, even when the situation seems chaotic. I can give you peace that you are living your life purpose. I can protect you from further harm. Your prayer should be the one of the Christ, (what He said on cross).

When you live out your life purpose, no matter how difficult it may seem at times, you will find an inner peace. You will know that all is well, even when others around you do not view it in the same light. Others may state how terrible your illness is, or how sad your circumstances are, but you will know that all is well. All is going along, according to the plan for your life. This kind of inner peace will emanate within your body and soul. Every angel will assist you in attaining this level of peace, if you simply ask for it.

There have been wonderful models on your earth, people who have been persecuted and had calmness and stillness within their souls. They were not resistant to the outcome, but accepting of it. Whenever you live through a situation where there seems to be no other possibility, then you will know it is part of your life plan. The calmness will be within you.

We are always with you. We watch you and we know you. There is not anything we will do, if it is for the highest good. If you make a request that we cannot fulfill, we will still answer you, but it will be in a different way.

Let me give you an example. Often, we hear the prayer that you do not want someone you love to die, in the physical body. If it is time for the person to die, and the person has accepted this, the passing will be peaceful and calm. If it is time and the person is still fighting this possibility, the journey may have its struggles. But, this is for that person's soul growth. Your prayer should be that the person dying finds peace and knows love through his transition time. You are not able to see the whole picture on your side. You do not see the whole picture as we can. This is your lesson in trust and faith. When you pray for the highest good of all, then the passing will be exactly what the soul needs. You do not always know the best outcome, but faith will manifest the best outcome for that person's soul.

Please mull over this teaching. Pray for the highest good, not the outcome that you think seems best. We are here to support you, not to grant you every wish and desire that you may have.

It is important that you understand this way of thinking. Your life will be in harmony with the spiritual realms, with the Divine way of thinking.

May God bless you, every moment of your lives.

Final Message One Voice

One Voice

We are speaking to you as a group. We are blending our voices together to send this one message to you: Let go and let God.

We know this phrase is known to many of you. It is full of wisdom. It is talking about the releasing of old ideas, beliefs and attitudes. It is releasing them so that you can live in Love and Light.

When you hold onto old beliefs, that do not serve you, you are blocking Light coming into your life. It is like a roadblock and nothing new can come into your lives. Let go and let God means ridding yourself of false beliefs and attitudes that are based in fear.

When these beliefs and emotions are released, then new beliefs and emotions will come into your life. You will be motivated by love, and not fear. That is a shift in your thinking, which results in a shift in your entire being. This love will grow within you, and it will be spread onto others in your world.

It is vitally important that all people shift from fear into love. It begins with you. You are the only person who has control over your own thoughts and feelings. No one else can control it, and we choose not to. That is your own free will. As you grow in understanding of this Truth, you will only want to live in love. It is so much more pleasing than living in fear. Fear begets more fear. Love begets more love.

When you let go, you create space for God, for Love, in your lives. It is difficult, if not impossible, to live in fear and love at the same time. Some of you are doing that as you are living in the struggle of releasing fear and striving to live in love simultaneously. This takes much, much energy. It is a process, and you can win the struggle. Whenever you think or feel fear, send it to the Light. It will be gone. Then, ask for Love and Light to fill that space in your hearts. It will be done.

We love you. We want only the best for you. We urge you to grow more in Spirit and in Love. We also ask you not to forget to relax and to play. This restores your energies and then you are able to expend more energy into loving thoughts and actions. We will assist you along the way.

We express our gratitude to you for working with us, at all times. We know you are busy in your earthly lives, although you could release some of these things that make you feel too busy. Do not forget to take time away from your work, and your tv's and games, and spend quiet time. Quiet is very important to the restoration of your energy base.

We are always here for you. Ask for our assistance and it will be given. Always. We love you and we guide you. We send you our peace.

Amen.

The Archangels are always present and ready to help and support us – all we have to do is ask. These channeled teachings from seven Archangels – Metatron, Raphael, Zadkiel, Ariel, Uriel, Gabriel and Michael - are both timely and timeless. The Archangels address several problems in today's world, as well as impart teachings relevant to all eras on Mother Earth. The messages resonate with the Truth already existing within our hearts and souls. We are reminded to remember these essential Truths.

About Deborah Lloyd

Deborah Lloyd is a Usui and Karuna® Reiki Master, a certified holistic therapy practitioner and a hospice social worker, in Asheville, North Carolina. She also wrote the story of her personal healing journey in the book, Believe and it is True: A Story of Healing and Life Lessons. She is a co-author of Reiki 101: 101 Answers for Your Reiki Questions, published by Reiki Rays. Additionally, she is one of the contributing article writers for reikirays.com.

Printed in Poland
by Amazon Fulfillment
Poland Sp. z o.o., Wrocław